DEDICATION

God is the only Giver of wisdom, knowledge and understanding. I appreciate Him for giving me the opportunity to complete this book to Him all glory.

INTRODUCTION

Marriage can be unpredictable. It is a journey that requires a lot of patience and endurance. Cases of marriage breakups are rampant in our society and this must be addressed to avoid a recurrence in the lives of our youths that are preparing for marriage. This book focuses on three major words - Relationship, Trust, and Love.

Before any commitment to a relationship, there must have been observations and interaction with the person to a great extent. Dating a would-be spouse should last for a minimum period of one and a half years. This will make you know each other to an extent though it does not give 100% guarantee, but it will help you in the future after marriage. Without relationship marriage can crash at any time.

Building Trust and Love before Marriage is crucial. A marriage without trust and love is like planting crops on the rock; the roots of the planted crops will not penetrate deeply and will wither off within a short time. I want to admonish you from my own experience in the journey of marriage. Nobody can confidently say that his or her marriage is perfect; it is the help and the grace of God that sustains marriages.

Patiently read this book and I assure you, after reading it, you will readily recommend this book to your friends and families - both home and abroad.

ACKNOWLEDGEMENT

My appreciation goes to God for the opportunity given me to write this book and to those who have devoted time and energy towards the production of this book. God in His mercy will abundantly reward you.

About the Author

Sowunmi Samuel is a clergyman, a seasoned marriage counselor and a freelance writer from Nigeria. He has passion for writing books on marriage counseling. His first book titled "Reason for Marriage Breakdown and The Way Out" was published in 2013 and over 7,000 copies were sold offline. He has zeal for youth empowerment and has been a guest speaker in many conferences, churches and seminars.

Sowunmi Samuel founded Getupdatenaija.com, a reputable site that conveys high-class digital marketing to Africa and beyond. Getupdatenaija.com is a platform for reading stimulating news and innovative articles that will constantly arouse your interest to frequently visit our site.

Visit www.getupdatenaija.com for news an articles
Whatsapp +234 70378524

About the Book

The purpose of this book is to guide about-to-wed Sisters and Brothers. Do not rush to marriage. Marriage is a journey which you must not quite, it is ordained by God, is not what anybody can just jump into you must study your partner before dating/propose each other.

There are many single mothers in our community today because of promiscuity and failure to patiently search and wait for God's will for their lives.

The consequence of this act is having unwanted pregnancy, sustaining moral scars and experiencing heartaches.

Kindly digest this book thoroughly for both spiritual and physical guide on how to plan for and have a successful marriage.

Note

This book is not for commercial gain interest or anybody should not reprint part of the book for financial gain. You are free to download this book at any convenient time. Invite your friend family relatives to visit our site to download the book free.

CONTENT

Page

CHAPTER ONE
Don't Rush into Marriage

Marriage is what every adolescent looks forward to at a certain age in life. This exhilarating and honorable occasion is better experienced than explained. Marriage is what every youngster should desire and never handle carelessly. I give glory to God who has sustained my wedding till today; though no marriage is hundred percent perfect, but with the help of God, we can weather every storm in marriage. My marriage has been a blessing in all ramifications; nonetheless, in every marriage, there are hurdles to cross as everything will not always be rosy; even life itself is not a bed of roses. Marriage, being a lifetime project, requires adequate planning. There are steps to take when venturing into marital partnership. Though God is our Master Planner and has given us wisdom to plan for our future, failure on our part to plan appropriately is tantamount to planning to fail and being wrecked in life.

Of a fact, wedding plan is not a child's play considering the fact that the would-be spouses must have developed spiritually, physically, socially and psychologically. Also, there must be emotional maturity, financial independence (ability to manage income and expenditure expertly), secured secular status, and so on. All these are tasking and worse still, divorce as the aftermath realization of a wrong marriage, is deadlier.

Eagerness to enter into marriage without proper planning exposes you to the danger of partnering with the wrong person. If you rush into marriage with someone, you run the risk of missing the right person with whom you would have been a better match with and thereby miss the perfect will of God for your life. Any God-ordained marital partner will be a soul-mate who would be willing to patiently endure the waiting period of planning and preparation, till the consummation of the wedding ceremony after which you are liable to spend the rest of your lives together. If your would-be spouse is too much in a haste to get married, then take caution and retrace your steps in order to diligently seek out someone that is patient.

Rushing to get married simply because of loneliness is a wrong notion as you tend to settle with an incompatible partner. Don't let your desperation blindfold you to the obvious red flags, because what you settle for is ultimately what you will get. It takes a long time, possibly years, to really get to know the person that you are dating. Tying the nuptial knot hastily (within few months of meeting each other) may deprive you the opportunity of knowing yourselves in-depth. Though initially it could be interesting, but it won't take long after marriage that you will realize or detect your incompatibility with each other and this will be difficult to deal with as you have signed a legal bond already.

Another costly consequence of being desperate to get married is; tendency of the other partner to tactfully withdraw. If you are pressuring your partner into marriage when he/she is not ready, then you are not mature enough to be in a relationship. Being aggressive and pushy about spending the rest of your lives together is not going to sweeten the pot for him/her. It is either slow down or run for the hills.

Breaking up is hard to do, but divorce is harder as it involves a lot of heartaches, paperwork, lawyers, strife, and somewhat time consuming. Breaking that contract is even more hellish than the heartbreak.

CHAPTER TWO
My Experiences before Wedding and after Wedding

Nobody can predict the future of your marriage for you. Marriage is white and black; yes, I reiterate it, marriage is white and black. When you look at the sky you can see that it is not completely white but has a mixture of blue and black; that can be likened to marriage.

I met my wife during the church youth convocation and our courtship lasted for two years and three months. During our courtship, we thought we had understood each other but sincerely, experiences taught us better after marriage. The first misunderstanding between us came up after two years and it nearly broke up our marriage. I married at the age of twenty-eight years while my wife was twenty-six years. What was the bone of contention? I was preparing to launch into a full time ministry but unknown to me, my wife was not in support of such but she was reluctant to bear her mind to me on the issue.

So when it was barely a month to launch the ministry, she protested and said "MD (my dear), we did not sign any agreement that you will become a full time minister. You are a publisher and I want you to focus on your profession". She reaffirmed that we never discussed anything about a full time ministry during courtship. The question is, "Why did she refuse?" What was wrong with her action and statement? I felt so bad that I started to pray that God should minister to her. It was over a year before she succumbed, based on her reason which I will not divulge on this platform, but I learnt my lesson; if I had told her during courtship, there would have been no problem. I apologized to her and the matter was amicably settled. In fact, God has used my wife mightily in my ministry.

My counsel to all youths, especially those about to wed is not to rush into marriage but know your partner to an extent; the long period of courtship notwithstanding, is never enough to explore each other. There must be no communication gap between the two of you. Lack of communication during the courtship can lead to insincerity; let there be openness between you and earn the trust of each other. Love your partner sincerely and do not argue with each other; if there is any occasion for offence, let there be earnest forgiveness.

CHAPTER THREE
Disadvantages of Starting Relationship at the Wrong Time

The best dating relationships develop out of great friendships. Finding a <u>meaningful relationship</u> takes time. While you spend time getting to know someone as a friend, you are able to explore that person, looking for the traits that connote an appropriate friendship. There is not a more valuable friend to a dating relationship than time. But sadly, many people are overridden by their emotions; hence, they throw caution into the air and rashly conclude that they are in love. In all honesty, is that love really?

Impatience is a sure sign of relational immaturity that will <u>lead to hurt</u> unimaginably. The truth is, the best dating <u>relationships</u> develop out of great friendships, and therefore, it must not be rushed into. Meeting someone who suddenly makes you feel alive and loved is very exciting; you may think no one has ever made you feel like this and you can't help but be amazed at the chemistry, or current that is running between you and this new love. Many <u>relationships</u> start this way. But sadly, those involved do not take time to get to know each other before jumping into something serious. Often, these kinds of relationships built on infatuation die as quickly as they spring up. The truth is this, the urgent feeling and <u>intensity or strong attraction</u> toward the other person is not necessarily a reliable indicator of whether you are in love or that you should immediately dive into a serious dating relationship.

People don't fall in love; they fall into hole. When you rush into a romantic <u>relationship</u>, you tend to:

- Say things you do not mean.
- Make promises you cannot keep.
- Dig a hole that is hard to get out of.

- Arouse expectations you cannot fulfill.

- Trust your feelings rather than the truth.

- Find it easy to make wrong choices.

- Do not give the relationship time to grow in a healthy way.

- Keep looking for more emotional thrills and then invite boredom into the relationship, where everything normal starts to feel boring.

- End up spending too much time with the one you are dating, and excluding your friends.

- Believe in the myth of love at first sight; there is no such thing, rather there is good chemistry at first sight. People do not fall in love; rather, they fall into the hole of captivity.

<u>Strong relationships</u> develop slowly overtime with much hard work and commitment. The smooth picture of relationships we see between some men and women are built on good foundation; that is why they enjoy themselves. I would also advise you to take time to pray, asking God to guide you as you consider a relationship with someone. This is an important decision that involves your heart. <u>God wants to guide you</u> and protect you; so, ask Him!

CHAPTER FOUR
Investigate Before You Date Each Other

Before you say yes to any marriage proposal, spiritual searching is paramount in this journey because if you miss it from the onset, you cannot adjust the journey along the way. Remember, before you sign your marriage contract of 'till death do us part', do a thorough spiritual searching. Some have missed their journey of relationship and that is why divorce is rampant today.

Know God experientially and put Him first in all you do. It is your knowledge of God that will spur you into the prayer of faith to seek His face in the choice of a life partner. On your own, you are likely to make mistakes in the choice of a life partner; there is a tendency to be carried away with facial beauty or tailor-made beauty. Physical appearance can be deceitful as human beings can perfectly package themselves in pretense; but God, who is the perfect Match-Maker, the One who has the calendar of your life in His hand and who wishes you well, will lead you to the rightful partner.

I was in youth's convocation years back, listening to a message on "Let the Holy Spirit Speak to You". The Lady Minister narrated her experience in the course of choosing a life partner. According to her, there was a particular man who pestered her for dating. The man though naturally caring, she refused vehemently because of a trait she noticed in him. After much pressure, she made up her mind and decided to pay the man a visit but the preceding night to the day she planned to visit this man, she had a dream and saw the man drinking alcohol. She confronted him in the dream, querying him why he would be drinking if he were born again; the man upon hearing this turned his back to her and hid the drink. On further attempt to speak with him in the dream, she woke up from her sleep. Immediately after she woke up, a voice asked her thus, "Have you seen the picture of the man you want to visit?"

God speaks to everyone in different ways if we allow the Holy Spirit to take control of our lives. The lady narrated how she met her husband also through a dream; God showed her the character of her life partner before she gave her consent.

(b)   **Do Physical and Medical Searching**

It is not everything that glitters that is gold. Do not date a partner because of outer beauty; rather, give inner beauty the preference. It is advisable for a man to look out for diligence in a woman, never settle for a lazy woman who will not be able to hygienically keep the home but will subject you to the temptation of having a house-help carry out virtually all domestic chores at home. Likewise, a woman must consider the capability of a man she intends to marry as regards shouldering the basic responsibilities at home as the would-be head of the union. It is expedient that both partners also consider the status of each other in respect of HIV TEST and Genotype compatibility.

GENOTYPE COMPATIBILITY

Genotype can be simply defined as the genetic constitution of an individual organism.   This is different from your phenotype which is a description of your actual physical characteristics. It is imperative to know your genotype before you say "yes" to that handsome guy or to that beautiful lady whom you wish to spend the rest of your life with or if you are in a relationship in which there are chances of conception.

The problem to avoid with genotype compatibility for intending couples is the sickle cell disease (a recessive disorder) - a very serious medical condition with high prevalence rates in Africa, south of the Sahara.

Types of Genotype

The genotypes in humans are AA, AS, AC, and SS. They refer to the hemoglobin gene constituents on the red blood cells. AC is rare whereas AS + AC are abnormal.

Genotype Compatibility Chart

Study this table below carefully:

AA + AA	=	AA,	AA,	AA,	AA	(Excellent)
AA + AS	=	AA,	AS,	AA,	AS	(Good)
AA + SS	–	AS,	AS,	AS,	AS	(Fair)
AA + AC	=	AA,	AA,	AA,	AC	(Good)
AS + AS	=	AA,	AS,	AS,	SS	(Very Bad)
AS + SS	=	AS,	SS,	SS,	SS	(Very Bad)
AS + AC	=	AA,	AC,	AS,	SS	(Bad; Advice needed)
SS + SS	=	SS,	SS,	SS,	SS	(Very Bad)
AC + SS	=	AS,	AS,	SS,	SS	(Very Bad)
AC + AC	=	AA,	AC,	AC,	SS	(Bad; Advice needed)

Compatible genotypes for marriage are:

AA marries an AA. That is the best compatible. That way you save your future children the worry about genotype compatibility.

AA marries an AS. You will end up having children with AA and AS which is good. But sometimes if you are not lucky, all the children will be AS which limits their choice of partners.

AS and AS should not marry, there is every chance of having a child with SS.

AS and SS should not think of marrying each other.

Finally, SS and SS must not marry themselves since their offspring will definitely take after them, having the sickle cell disease.

Solution

The only remedy to change the genotype is the Bone Marrow Transplant (BMT). It has been proven to be the only promising permanent cure to SS, SC, and CC; however, it is new, very expensive and cannot be done in any part of Africa. It also carries some risks. (*American University of Nigeria website Google date: 13 June, 2020*).

(c)   **Know Each Other's Parents**

It is not out of the way to know each other's parents by the sixth or seventh month after giving your consent to be in a relationship. This is expedient because after knowing God's leading in marriage, your parents are next and they actually have the final say as regards both of you marrying yourselves. I believe if the initial investigation which I call spiritual searching was made biblically, then you will not have any problem with both parents.

CHAPTER FIVE
Keep Your Relationship Healthy

Every relationship is unique, and people come together for different reasons. Part of what defines a healthy relationship is sharing a common goal for exactly what you want the relationship to be and where you want it to go. And that is something you will only know by relating with your partner in honesty. However, there are some characteristics that most healthy relationships have in common. Knowing these basic principles can help keep your relationship meaningful, fulfilling and exciting; whatever the goals that you are working towards or challenge that both of you are facing.

Good communication is crucial to a healthy relationship. When you experience a positive emotional connection with your partner, you feel safe, happy and comfortable to express your needs, fears, and desire thereby increasing the trust and thus strengthen the bond between you. When people stop communicating well, they stop relating well, and times of change or stress can really bring out the disconnection. This may sound simplistic, but as long as you are communicating, you can usually work through whatever problems you are facing.

You each make the other feel loved and emotionally fulfilled. There is a difference between being loved and *feeling* loved. When you feel loved, it makes you feel accepted and valued by your partner, like someone truly gets you. Some relationships get stuck in peaceful coexistence, but without the partners truly relating to each other emotionally. While the union may seem stable on the surface, a lack of ongoing involvement and emotional connection serves only to add distance between two people.

While a great deal of emphasis in our society is put on talking, if you can learn to listen in a way that makes another person feel valued and understood, you can build a deeper, stronger connection between you. There is a big difference between listening in this way and simply hearing. When you really listen—when you are engaged with what is being said—you will hear the subtle intonations in your partner's voice that tells you how they are really feeling and the emotions they are trying to communicate. Being a good listener does not mean you have to agree with your partner or change your mind. But it will help you find common points of view that can help you to resolve conflict.

Knowing what is truly important to your partner can go a long way towards building goodwill and an atmosphere of compromise. On the flip side, it is also important for your partner to recognize your wants and for you to state them clearly. Constantly giving to others at the expense of your own needs will only build resentment and anger.

If you approach your partner with the attitude that things have to be your way, it will be difficult to reach a compromise. Sometimes this attitude comes from not having your needs met while younger, or it could be years of accumulated resentment in the relationship reaching a boiling point. It is alright to have strong convictions about something, but your partner deserves to be heard as well. Be respectful of the other person's viewpoint.

Conflict is inevitable in any relationship, but to keep a relationship strong, both people need to feel they have been heard. The goal is not to win but to maintain and strengthen the relationship. Keep the focus on the issue at hand and respect the other person. Do not start arguments over things that cannot be changed, resolving conflict is impossible if you are unwilling or unable to forgive others. Take a few minutes to relieve stress and calm down before you say or do something you will regret. Always remember that you are arguing with the person you love. If you cannot come to an agreement, agree to disagree. It takes two people to keep an argument going. If a conflict is going nowhere, you can choose to disengage and move on.

CHAPTER SIX
Positive and Negative Effects of Long or Short Dating

The purpose of this book is to guide the about-to-wed Sisters and Brothers. There are positive and negative effects of long and short dating. I will suggest that minimum of one and half years is good for both couple to have 40% understanding of each other while two years is adequate for couples who are not in a hurry to wed.

I have witnessed dating relationship of three months and six months respectively and till date, the couples are living together in peace. It depends on their maturity but to be sincere, if dating time is long, sometimes it can lead to separation but I must reiterate the fact that you must understand your partner at the extent of 40% at least, before you go into marriage. It is a bitter truth that you can never know your spouse 100% all through your lifetime but you must learn how to manage your affairs and tolerate each other.

Causes of Long Dating

Age

Age difference between a man and a lady who intend to get married must not be wide apart. For instance, if a lady is twenty-one years of age while her partner is thirty-one years old, this wide range in age can cause long dating in that the man will have to wait for the lady to accomplish the basic achievements in life such as academic pursuit among others before settling for marriage. Therefore, it is very important to consider the age barrier before going into relationship.

Distant from Each Other

When a couple that intends to get married are distant from each other, such as living in two different countries, with the tiring processing protocols to be observed, then their coming together in wedlock will be delayed and this is not too comfortable.

Transfer from Workplace

In a relationship where one of the would-be couple is being frequently transferred from his or her workplace, such a relationship will be affected as the non-availability of the other partner will hamper the smooth preparation for their wedding. Though it is important to be gainfully employed so as to meet the needs of the family in the nearest future, yet, it is also essential that proper planning be made in view of this major issue and to work out a suitable plan.

High-class Ladies

If your taste is high as a lady, subjecting your partner to the hurdle of meeting all your needs before you agree to marry him, then know that you are likely to have a long dating time in a bid for the man to run around to get your needs met or you might out-rightly lose such partner if your demands are too many or too high beyond his financial capability. A lady who fortunately has a well to do partner that is gainfully employed; do not necessarily have to siphon him before she is taken care of during dating and after marriage. Be wary of what you subject your partner to as a wise partner.

Causes of Short Dating

Disappointments

Past relationship disappointments can engender desperation to tie the nuptial knot within a very short time; they are ready to do everything humanly possible not to let go of their current partners. Relationship disappointment has given deadly blows to some that they either eventually get deranged or decide to remain single but some smart victims of such bitter experiences will tactfully settle for a short dating period and get married within few months to secure such relationships.

Nonchalant Attitude

According to grammarphobia blog, the Oxford English Dictionary explains *nonchalant* to have been borrowed from French sometime before 1734 to mean "*neglect* or *despise*". I deliberately use this word to describe those ladies who are proud and make high demands from their partners. After wasting many years and opportunities, they become stigmatized as 'single old ladies' and out of desperation and frustration, they grab any opportunity that comes their ways eventually and get married within a short time. My word of advice for the young ladies who are still below age thirty is never to allow nonchalant attitude to set them back in marriage.

Spiritual Delay

Those that have experienced spiritual delay do not waste time in dating. As soon as they get into a relationship, they consummate such within a short period.

Physical Disability

Those who have physical challenges as a result of accident or even from birth, it could be a young man or a young woman, they do not waste time in long dating;

rather, they settled down as quickly as the opportunity to get married comes their ways and move on in life.

CHAPTER SEVEN
Avoid Sex During Dating Period

To be sincere, sex is not for young men and young ladies but an exclusive preserve for married couples. This may sound absurd to you but this is a bitter pill that must be swallowed. Have you come to think of it that after messing up your life with an opposite sex, you might end up not getting married eventually. Then how do you look at yourselves in the future after you have parted? Some young men demand for sex during their relationship as proof of love and if the ladies deny them, they feel not loved. This is wrong. Any sexual gratification outside marriage is against the will of God and outright disobedience to Him.

Sex is not a proof of love. To buttress this fact, come to think of it; can you justify that all men that sleep with prostitutes are in love with them? Also, sexual attraction is different from filial love as it is not acceptable for siblings to get involved in sexual relationship as a proof of love. Married couples do not have sex merely to prove their love; rather, they have sex as a mandatory part of their marital obligations both for procreation and pleasure.

As a marriage counselor, I have seen instances where things have fallen apart between couples – the wife denied the husband sex and the husband have to force her to gratify his sexual desire. Can such instance of selfish sexual gratification be regarded as true love? Once again, I reiterate the assertion that premarital sex is wrong. Sex intimacy is a blood covenant that involves body, soul, and spirit. Do you want your soul and spirit to be tied to somebody who is not going to marry you? In summary, sex is between husband and wife, not for young men and young ladies.

One of the greatest headaches of many young ladies in relationship is the issue of sex. It has turned into a mystery for many ladies, thinking what they feel for a particular guy is true love. You meet a guy, he takes you out; He had great sex with you, it was like heaven to you. He makes you feel happy because you enjoyed him so much that you start assuming both of you are meant to be together as husband and wife. You start dreaming of your future with him while he was just having fun. Your feelings for him have blindfolded you from seeing things from the reality point of view.

You find yourself infatuated with him just because you do not want to feel used and dumped. Sometimes you need to sit down and ask yourself these pertinent questions: What do I really love about this guy? Do I see Christ in him? Is he a guy I can boldly take to my parents and my pastor? Can I introduce him as my husband to people who are responsible? You know the guy is not capable of being a good husband and father; yet you offer yourself to him. Sometimes you need to differentiate between what you just feel and what you really deserve.

Don't start dreaming of your future with a guy who is just catching his fun. Don't attach a permanent feeling to a temporal person. Don't open up your heart to a guy who doesn't open his bible. Stop chasing after a guy who doesn't chase after God's word. Your relationship with him/her should be for a purpose, define your relationship, know where it's heading to. Someone that truly loves you can never demand for sex before marriage, engagement ring doesn't determine marriage, introducing you to his friends doesn't determine marriage. Ladies be wise.

CHAPTER EIGHT
The Essence of Maturity is Core

Apply Maturity to your relationship in the following ways:

 (a)   **Spiritual Maturity**

(b)   **Physical Maturity (Trust and Love)**

(c)   **Effective Communication Maturity**

Spiritual Maturity

I want to explain maturity in three ways. Spiritual maturity doesn't happen overnight. It is a process. A lot of couples wish they were closer spiritually; this makes sense since marriage is first and foremost a spiritual relationship. A marriage that invites Jesus into it will be stronger than the one that leaves Him out.

 As you continue your relationship you have to work toward this:

Worship together

There is nothing wrong with worshiping with each other, when you do this, you are inviting God into your journey, but do not let it turn into an obstacle that keeps you from growing together spiritually.

Meditate on the Word of God

Find time to read and meditate on the word of God as this will build your faith in God.

Pray together

Prayer is like the spiritual glue of marriage. Since most relationships live and die on communication, it makes sense that this is a key ingredient to a successful marriage. When you pray with your spouse, your heart is on display and you may feel vulnerable, which is not always easy. But you will be surprised by how much you can grow together from this simple process.

Physical maturity

Starting a relationship with someone just because you think being single will make you feel lonely, bored, or miserable is totally wrong. That is not the main reason why you should commit your time and attention to someone.

Physical maturity is the age and appearance of the person you want to date. Is he or she physically mature? Do not be surprised that some girls are between ten to fifteen years and they look like twenty-five to thirty years because they have fast growth and they are rushing and pushing for marriage. Wisdom is not by age don't quote me wrong. An underage wife is immature to handle the intricacies of childbirth and child training. Also, an immature mother can have complications during delivery hence; don't settle for underage regardless of the big stature of the young lady.

Effective Communication maturity

There is power in our tongues. Effective communication is about how you conduct yourself; there is a correlation between responsibility and maturity, but note that it is not responsibility that defines maturity; rather, it is maturity that allows for a responsible behavior.

When it comes to defining real effective communication, here are a few signs to look for:

Ability to Communicate

One misconception about communication is that you have to do a lot of it to be effective. Effective communication requires more listening than speaking. It also requires a certain level of thought before speaking. As spouses, you have to study each other and learn to communicate appropriately. To enjoy your marriage, keep in mind that when you are communicating with your partner, quantity is not quality, what you speak out will determine the response to your statement. So, choose your words and don't just talk anyhow.

We all have our own ideas and opinions, no matter how concise they may be, someone will always argue against what you say. Real maturity is the ability to debate your point without getting defensive. At some points, you have to be able to tell your partner, "We will agree to disagree." That does not involve insulting each other; you should accord your partner the same respect you want from him/or her as regards your opinions no matter how wrong it looks.

Complete Self-Acceptance

This is the ability to realize your virtues as well as your flaws; to appreciate your virtues and deal with your flaws constructively. There is a very distinct and cyclical nature between knowing yourself and trusting yourself. You have to first know yourself to be able to trust yourself – good or bad. If you know what your strengths and weaknesses are, you can appropriately trust yourself to deal with anything that involves those strengths and weaknesses.

Consciousness

Consciousness is synonymous with awareness, and that is a pretty good correlation to make. Being conscious does not just involve you and the opposite sex, it entails being aware of everyone around you. It is great to be fully aware of your own emotional state, situation, and general goings-on in your own life. But being completely ignorant of everyone around you is like walking through life with a box on your head. A huge part of maturity goes back to that "being responsible" thing. One thing we are all responsible for, to a point, is the people around us.

Ability to Accommodate versus Arguing

People have different ideas when it comes to just about anything in life. As you mature, you begin to realize that sometimes your idea is not the absolute best. It is a matter of compromise. You have to be able to set your ego aside to be able to accept outside input, and use it effectively.

Personal Growth is a Pursuit, not a Task

A sign of real maturity is your willingness to work on who you are as a person. When you are immature, you assume that you are the best that you can be. Your egos will convince you that there is nothing to "fix". The problem with this mentality is, not seeing anything that is "broken" for you to improve yourself.

A relationship is strengthened by the level of communication between the people involved because communication is the basis of life. Communication gap during relationship could lead to the death of that relationship. Do not find it difficult to use the phrases such as 'Am sorry', 'Forgive me', 'Please', 'Thank you', 'I love you'. Speak the truth in love, do not raise your voice at each other; share details, and don't repeat issues especially past one; allow for reaction and feedback, learn timing and use the maturity phrases.

CHAPTER NINE
Do Not Hide Your Past from Each Other

No one is an epitome of perfection; hence, there is no perfect partner. A lot of things might have gone wrong before you met your partner; take your time to study him/her, know the appropriate time to tell him/her your past mistakes, especially the complicated ones. Do not be secretive as this can have adverse effect on your marriage in the future.

It is advisable to open up to each other at the early stage of your relationship for your partner to decide either to go ahead with the relationship or to call it quit if he/she is not comfortable with your past. But if God is in the relationship, no matter how ugly the past has been, there will be continuity of the relationship that will be consummated in holy wedlock eventually.

The ugly past should not be allowed to jeopardize or overrule your relationship. For instance, if a lady was promiscuous in the past and she opens up to her would-be husband, this should not serve as a license to abuse such a lady or to make her feel bad, rather, her courageous confession should be appreciated. Meanwhile, the loss of virginity in male cannot be easily detected unlike ladies except such a young man opens up. Yet, for the sake of a healthy relationship, it is advisable that there be mutual openness and understanding and let holiness be your watchword all through the dating period. Also, any sexual intimacy should be reserved till when you legally sign the contract to be husband and wife for life.

CHAPTER TEN
Let Your Partner Know Your Weaknesses

It is not disputable that our strength is in God. But humanly speaking, despite our strength, we all have our weaknesses as well which cut across both physical and spiritual. Your partner's weakness must not be used as an avenue to relegate or belittle him/her; instead, there must be understanding and tolerance at the display of such.

By the grace of God, I am lucky to have married an enterprising woman who is an expert in culinary and not lazy in her work place but in case your wife is not good in the kitchen, all she knows how to cook is to boil white rice or indomie noodles, such a wife must have been worked on during courtship by tactfully connecting her to experienced women who are good homemakers to train her in the required skills to becoming a virtuous woman, before you go into marriage. If you really love her, you see it as a weak point in her that needs to be corrected and this should not be allowed to have a bearing on your relationship.

The weak point of many men in Africa is laziness in prayer. Before you disagree with this statement, let us take a look at the statistics of men readily available in the church service. In all sincerity, the population of women is always double if not more than that of the men. In view of this fact, the onus lies on our women to systematically teach their spouses the importance of communicating with God in prayer for the success of their homes.

CHAPTER ELEVEN
Planning for Your Matrimonial Home

When planning for your matrimonial home, the followings must be put into consideration:

(a)   Build Your Faith in God

(b)   Financial Planning

(c)   Child Bearing

(d)   Plan for Your Old Age

Above all, planning for your matrimonial home is very important. Some couples only plan for their wedding (a day ceremony) and in their bid to make the event a memorable one, they opt for loan because they want to impress their families and friends. There is nothing bad to invite family and friend to your wedding, to satisfy them with drinks and food among other things, but this must be done moderately and according to your financial capacity.

Spending a lot of money for a day ceremony is going to affect the marital journey. Please don't quote me wrong, most especially ladies, if your demand is higher than what your fiancé earns or can afford, and all what you crave for is flamboyant wedding; this will negatively affect your home after marriage. It is expedient that you are frugal in spending not only before wedding but also in managing your home after the wedding ceremony when there will be varieties of responsibilities and commitments.

I will talk on four major things you must have good plan in preparation for your matrimonial home.

Build your faith in God: Both of you must put God first in whatever you are doing. Let God be the foundation and the pillar of everything you want to do. Always communicate with God in your prayer and seek for advice from competent counselor. Let God be your alpha and omega.

Financial planning: This is a major issue in your matrimonial home. As I said earlier, in preparation for wedding ceremony, there must be moderation. Your capital must have budget plan such as:

- Paying for house rent
- Paying for utility bills
- Provide for house needs
- How to pay for children school fees
- Car maintenance
- Saving for any other project ahead of you

All what I mentioned above are the responsibilities of a good husband but it is not out of place if a good wife supports her husband. If a woman truly loves her husband, she must not allow the financial responsibility of the home to weigh the man down. Remember the wise saying that beside a successful man is a good woman.

Child bearing: Do you know that you have to plan for this? Two of you must agree on how many children you will have. Feeding and to give a child sound education is very expensive. It is not bad to have many children inasmuch as your income can commensurate their required care. But my advice for you is to minimize child bearing to the level of your income.

Plan for your old age: This is part of financial aspect that I mentioned above. You have to save money for old age. At your old age, your strength will reduce, you will not able to go up and down for daily needs. If you plan adequately for your old age, it will be of great advantage then.

CHAPTER TWELVE
Marry Legally

49

If a man takes advantage of any lady to become his wife without carrying out the proper marital rites, then their cohabitation is illegal.

Here are papers you need to back up your marriage:

Marriage is registered at a local public registry, which requires a Letter of Marriage Intention and payment of a fee go to your local public registry. Ask for the fee.

A person under 18 years of age, who wishes to register a marriage, is required to present a letter of consent from his or her parents (underage marriage is not advisable).

The registry will display the Letter of Marriage Intention for 21 days on a public notice board.

50

Provided that no objection to the intended marriage is made during the 21-days period, a couple may then register their marriage.

Birth certificates or official documents showing the ages of the couple are required together with the results of HIV and genotype tests.

If you intend to go for church wedding, you are qualified for this after you have received your marriage certificate.

Other Books by Sowunmi Samuel

1   Reason for Marriage Breakdown and the Way Out

2   Husband and Wife Roll for Effective Christian Home

3   The Causes of Polygamy in Christendom

4   Building Relationship Love and Trust before Marriage

5   Parental Roll to Their Children